thinkBIG:
there's no secret
to success

Dr. John A. King

Think Big: There's No Secret to Success

NEXT Foundation
www.nextfoundation.org

Office: 1-817-320-9591
Email: mel@nextfoundation.org
PO Box 1436
Grapevine, TX 76099

Copyright, 2017 by Dr. John A. King
All rights reserved.

Published by Next Foundation Press
ISBN 978-0-9965687-1-5

think
BIG
there's no secret to success

NEXT FOUNDATION PRESS

To the Back Deck Crew,

Thank You.

(Especially to member number 4 - she is really hot.)

I dedicate not only this book, but this whole next chapter of my life to the friendship and belief that helped get me back on my feet.

All the good bits are yours.

All the bits I stuck together with duct tape when no-one was looking—I take full responsibility for.

Here's to the Good Guys, we win....

John

CONTENTS

PREFACE 9

WHY THIS BOOK? 13

CH 1: there is no secret to success 15

CH 2: thoughts are things 25

CH 3: we become what we think about 41

CH 4: what is success? 73

CH 5: the power of persistence 83

CH 6: smile and enjoy the fire 109

CH 7: time to get real 119

MORE FROM DR. JOHN A. KING 133

IMAGE CREDITS 135

PREFACE

Next Foundation was established on this simple premise: if we could help facilitate the dreams of others, then we would achieve everything that we have purposed to do in terms of our positive impact on individuals, non-profits, and corporations.

For over 30 years, I spoke and presented in small country towns in outback Australia, thatched huts in Asia and the Pacific Islands, large auditoriums, conference centers and boardrooms across America and Europe.

I was blowing and going; life was good. My health was good. My family was good. Then in July 2008, something happened that would change my life forever. It was three o'clock in the afternoon; I believe it was a Thursday.

At the age of 45 (2008), I had total recall of the sexual abuse I suffered from around ages 4 to 16 by both my parents and their friends. When the memories that I had repressed all my life came back, the impact was overwhelming. The effect on my emotional, mental and relational life was completely devastating. (I talk about this more extensively on the No Working Title and Give Them A Voice Foundation websites.)

When I tried to find someone to talk to, I just couldn't. The traditional avenues of care were focused exclusively on women. I had nowhere to turn. I felt completely isolated. I realized that if I was ever going to lead a normal life again, I would have to figure out what normal was and then figure out how to inhabit the life I wanted.

Part of my process was coming to accept that I would never be "healed" from the memories of my past, that they would always be a part of me. I made the decision that I would allow them to refine me but never define me. If healing was never an option, then I would give myself to finding the tools I needed to manage the day to day effects that long term sexual abuse has on a person. I would turn my Post Traumatic Stress into Post Traumatic Strengths.

Every day I would rise and read, listen and search for just one more tool for my "Get Back in the Game" tool box (sounds way better than "Recovery" tool box). I was not trying to rehash someone else's book to make memes. I was desperately trying to find a way to get beyond surviving to reclaim a life lost and a future I felt was unfulfilled.

What I am trying to say is that these teachings are not theoretical. They actually work, and now I want to pass them on to you. I hope this book helps you with your journey as well. I hope you are challenged, excited and equipped to be the best version of you that you can possible be.

—Dr. Firstname

(You know, like Dr. Phil or Dr. Bob...apparently that's what you have to do. Also, you're supposed to wear a suit with no tie. Oh well. This is me in a beanie at the gym.)

CHAPTER 1
THERE IS NO SECRET TO SUCCESS

"We all have the extraordinary coded within us, waiting to be released."

—Jean Houston

In all honesty, there is no secret to success.

There is, however, a group of people who have overcome seemingly insurmountable odds, risen above circumstances and situations to do certain things that others don't. They have all applied principles that are discernible, teachable and repeatable. These principles can be learned today and applied tomorrow to develop similar traits and habits in your life. I know this to be true—I have done it.

All these extraordinary folks share a common attitude. They continually push forward beyond their circumstances or disabilities, and end up living a life beyond mediocrity or externally applied limits. Somewhere along the way, they all seemed to have decided that they want a life of achievement and personal impact. They want to live their lives fully in spite of what others would see as setbacks.

They found reasons to succeed, not excuses to fail.

I am firmly convinced that our lives are 10% what happens to us, and 90% how we respond to it.

Ted Engstrom once wrote, "Cripple him, and you have a Sir Walter Scott. Lock him in a prison cell, and you have a John Bunyan. Bury him in the snows of Valley Forge, and you have a

George Washington. Raise him in abject poverty, and you have an Abraham Lincoln. Subject him to bitter religious prejudice, and you have a Benjamin Disraeli. Strike him down with infantile paralysis, and he becomes Franklin D. Roosevelt. Call him a slow learner, 'retarded,' and write him off as uneducated, and you have an Albert Einstein."

For these people:

There were no excuses.

They were not victims.

They refused to be crybabies.

Fig. 1

They refused to succumb to paranoia, or become cultural or ethnic victims.

The indomitable heart of these over-comers marched on regardless of their circumstances.

Let's get one thing straight, right up front:

Life is tough, friend. It is not fair and sometimes it is just plan wrong. But you're not special or unique. The world is not plotting against you, it is rough for everyone. Problems and pain exist. They will always exist, but they must never be allowed to conquer the soul.

You may not like to hear this in a culture where the depths of our relational help comes from Pinterest, and we have limited our self-development to memes. But life just basically sucks at times, and there is nothing you can do about it but hang on and ride out the sucky-ness (yes, that is a word).

The commonalities that exist among this apparently elite group are not beyond the grasp of all of us. They are not elusive, they are hiding in plain sight. I haven't just taught them, I had to learn to live them—one day, one skill at a time.

What I want to do with this book (really this whole series of books) is to share some of the principles that were absolutely vital to me when the walls came tumbling down in my life in 2008.

I firmly believe that these principles can be learned and applied to any life, in any country or culture, at any time.

A SURVEY

Some years ago, I surveyed a group of leaders from various backgrounds. They were business leaders, church leaders, and community leaders. I asked them two simple questions, and I gave them twenty-five minutes to complete their answers.

The questions were:

1. What is the one thing you want to achieve in your life—the thing you want to spend the rest of your days doing?
2. What are three reasons you are not doing it, or three things that are keeping you back from your dream?

What surprised me the most was that the exercise was over in about twelve minutes. There was no hesitation from the group, just an articulation of the issues they already knew they faced.

Not one of the people I asked said that they did not have the ability to do what they wanted.

Not one of them said that they did not believe they had the capacity to do what they wanted.

Not one of them said that the economy or their ethnicity was to blame.

Every one of these people KNEW what it was they were supposed to do.

The one thing standing between them, their lifetime goals and ambitions, was themselves.

Here is a summary of the reasons they gave for not pursuing their passions in life:

- Personal discipline
- Living in the past
- Not really wanting it, just pretending to
- Fear of success
- Wasting time
- Procrastination
- Low self-esteem
- Lack of knowledge
- Fear of failure
- Lack of preparation
- Fear of what others might think

In essence, they saw their way of thinking and the lack of a prepared strategy as the greatest limitations to obtaining their goals.

My survey participants were not unique. I've found the same thing all around the world, with people from all walks of life. No matter who you are, if you have obstacles standing between you and your goals and ambitions, the process is the same.

In order to reposition yourself for your future, there are four major things you must address:

1. How you think

2. What you say

3. What you do

4. The company you keep

In the following chapters, I am going to address these areas in several ways. By the end of the book you will come to understand not only why these four areas are key, but what you need to be able to do to develop them in your life.

CHAPTER 2
THOUGHTS ARE THINGS

"Thinking is like loving and dying. Each of us must do it for himself."

—Josiah Royce

The very first principle I had to come to terms with when I was starting again was that the key to my future lay in my confession. I know it sounds like a gift shop bookmark, but it was vital for me. Life was so stinking bad; every day was a nightmare of self-doubt, self-judgement and a total, overwhelming sense of failure. I told you, it sucked.

During this time, I came to realize that I could see what was in me—the fear, the panic, etc.—by the words that came out of me. If I didn't change what was in me, there was no way I could change what came out of me, and consequently change the fruit of my life.

I didn't know where I was going, I just knew I didn't want to be "here" anymore. I needed to change what was in my head and my heart. Two reflections became the foundation for my growth and development going forward:

1. You become what you think about.

2. You have to pay a price for anything of value.

YOU HAVE TO SOW GOOD SEED INTO GOOD SOIL

My first degree is in Agriculture, sheep and pigs. (Perfect preparation for getting into the ministry later in life). I put myself through

college driving trucks and tractors in outback New South Wales, Australia.

We used to sow various crops at various times of the year—often oats in the spring and wheat in the summer.

At planting time, you never wanted to get your grains mixed up. If you had more than a certain percentage of the wrong crop mixed in, for example, oats in your wheat harvest, the harvest was deemed contaminated and you would not receive the maximum price from the grain buyers.

If a farmer didn't pay attention to the proper care and maintenance of his equipment, if he didn't clean it out properly after each use, or if he mingled the wrong seeds, what he reaped was not what he had hoped or planned to reap.

Lets assume the following things:

- the farmer has a good block of land
- it is well irrigated land
- it is fertile soil that has a proven potential

If all of these things are in place, then the land guarantees the farmer two things:

1. He will have to make a choice
2. Based on that choice he will get a reward.

The return that the farmer receives is predicated on the farmer's choice of seed and his care for the seed (sowing, fertilizing and watering). If the farmer sows the seed and cares for the crop then the farmer will reap what has been sown. Whatever the farmer puts into the land, the land might return to him 30, 60 or 100 percent, all dependent upon the quality of the seed and the care for it after sowing.

In a very real sense, the land is neutral. The land cannot tell the difference between the seeds sown. The land doesn't know if it is oats or wheat or weeds. The land will treat the seeds exactly the same; it will give each seed an opportunity to grow to its full potential.

The only difference will be in the harvest that it produces.

The farmer digs a hole and plants two seeds, one oats and one wheat. He then covers them up and he waters them both. The land will do what the land was designed to do; it will produce and bring forth fruit according to the seed planted.

Now, imagine that the farmer has planted both seeds with full knowledge that half his crop was oats and the other half was wheat. This wasn't an accidental thing, it was a deliberate thing.

The farmer can wish that the oats don't sprout. He can hope for only wheat to grow and be ripe for harvest. He can pray for his crop all that he wants, but the fate of the crop is already sealed because the seed will produce after its own kind. Once the seed is planted and watered, unless the sprouting plant is forcefully and deliberately removed, it will bear fruit. The fruit will be according to the seed; after the nature and after the character of the seed.

THE HUMAN MIND

Earl Nightingale suggested that the human mind was far more fertile ground and has far greater potential than any plot of land. He suggested that it works in the same manner: what you sow into the field of your mind will produce a physical crop in your life.

Another way of saying this:

Thoughts are things. You become what you think about.

One morning while reading the business section of the USA Today, I noticed two juxtaposed articles.

The first article was about two unemployed brothers. They had just won a million dollars from a super bowl advertisement they had created on their home computer for about two hundred dollars.

The other article was about another group of people who were fearful due to the condition of the economy, scared about the future and their jobs. The article described how they were all running out and selling their houses, rooming together or moving back in with their parents, just in case something bad happened to them economically.

Same paper, same day, same economy—two sets of people, each with two different mindsets. Both sowing different seeds in their minds, both reaping different crops for their lives.

THOUGHTS ARE THINGS. YOU BECOME WHAT YOU THINK ABOUT.

Someone is going to make a whole lot of money in this economy. Someone is going to come up with new business ideas and make enough money to leave an inheritance to their children's children in this economy. Others will huddle together fearfully waiting for the sky to fall.

The economy is not the determining factor in your financial success—you are!

I can hear your cries, "No, that's not true, that's just that televangelist rubbish! You sound like Fletch."

It doesn't matter what generation you live in, there will always be someone who will tell you that this economic downturn could be as bad as it was in the Great Depression.

Ok. So what if it is?

The Great Depression of 1929-1939 resulted in more people making their individual fortunes than at any other time in American history.

During the Great Depression there was 15% unemployment rate—tragic. However, that meant that 85% of the people had work. What are you going to focus on?

If you focus on failure, or on what happened the last time you tried this or that, or how your friend tried to start a business and failed, or how no one in your family has ever received a college education—if those are the seeds you are planting into the soil of your mind, or have been planted there by others—you are right, you will never do it.

You will never obtain it.

You will never succeed. Why? Because you will become what you think about.

ELEPHANT ON A CHAIN

If you've ever traveled through Asia, you have probably seen big, old elephants—huge—just standing in the middle of a crowded square, chained to a little stake by a very small chain.

I've looked at the size of the chain, and then the size of the elephant. I know that the elephant could easily pull out that stake and run off into the forest.

Yet it stands there, walking in circles around that little stake all day long. Why? How can something so big, so powerful, just stand there tied to a little stake? That's not what it was destined or designed for. What has happened to the wild, unfettered greatness that lies within its DNA? Why does it act like that? Why?

Because that it is all it has ever known. That is all it has come to expect of life

Fig. 2

When an elephant is young, they take a small chain and a little stake. They drive that stake into the ground and chain it there.

The baby elephant pulls and struggles, but because of its age and size, it cannot move the stake and the shackle never comes off its leg.

That elephant grows up expecting, believing, and experiencing the bondage of that chain. It never realizes that its own strength and ability to remove that chain has changed over time.

People are like that. They grow up a certain way. They are taught a certain thing. They are told that what they have and are experiencing is all they can expect out of life.

They get complacent and comfortable, and never bother to test the bondages and restrictions that make up their past. Even worse, some actually empower the chain by blaming the chain for their condition. They speak to the chain and tell it how it is holding them back.

Like the elephant, people hand over their future and potential to the chain and stake that bind them. They refuse to see the possibility of life without the bonds of culture, fear, poverty or sickness. They consign themselves to a hopeless, bound, restricted future.

Many people spend their whole lives without really flexing their muscles and re-envisioning who they are, based upon the REAL potential that lies within them.

They simply never break the chain.

You see, the elephant never thinks about freedom; the elephant only thinks about the chain. It is so focused on what it has never been able to do before, that it never tests boundaries or tries something different.

When I first read about the elephant I thought to myself, "That is ridiculous. That is crazy! Why doesn't it just break loose?"

But then I thought about the people that I have worked with—the clients, the companies, the churches, and the community groups. They are all great people, and they all have the same information available to them that everyone else has, but they are seeing no forward movement, they are seeing no change in themselves or their lives.

They hear the information that can set them free, read a book that stirs them up, attend a seminar where their questions are answered, yet there is no transformation.

Dr. Edward Miller, the dean of the medical school and CEO of the hospital at Johns Hopkins University made this incredible statement:

"If you look at people after coronary-artery bypass grafting two years later, 90% of them have not changed their lifestyle...."

These patients, regardless of the fact that their lives were at risk, stayed chained to old paradigms, doing the same things and getting the same results, one hamburger with fries at a time.

FROM INFORMATION TO TRANSFORMATION

People often spend their entire lives shackled by something that happened in their past. Many are bound up by what their dad said, what their mother did to them, or what a teacher told them.

FROM INFORMATION
TO TRANSFORMATION

They are shackled by what the doomsayers tell them about the future of the world and the economy.

In order for people to experience freedom from their past, information must become revelation, then only through application comes their transformation.

Those are the four steps: information, revelation, transformation, application. Four simple and doable keys to turning any life, business or organization around.

YOU VALUE WHAT YOU PAY FOR

Most people tend to place little value on what they have been given for free. People will value a house, a car, a book, or an outfit because they had to pay for them.

The money and effort they had to give in order to obtain something is why they spend so much time hovering over it, looking after it, or showing it off.

The things we do not pay for we do not seem to value so highly.

Before you start fighting with me about this statement, think about it.

Is it not true that anything that money can buy can be replaced? Conversely, anything that money cannot buy cannot be replaced?

ANYTHING THAT MONEY CAN BUY CAN BE REPLACED. ANYTHING THAT MONEY CANNOT BUY CANNOT BE REPLACED.

You cannot replace a friend. You cannot replace a marriage. You cannot replace time. You cannot replace your health. You cannot replace your mind. You cannot replace an opportunity.

We paid nothing for them; therefore we tend to put little value on them until they're gone. We take these things for granted.

CHAPTER 3
WE BECOME WHAT WE THINK ABOUT

"Whether you believe you can, or whether you believe you can't, you're right."

—Henry Ford

Fig. 3

YOU MUST THINK DIFFERENTLY TO LIVE DIFFERENTLY

So how do you change?

How do you become all that you can be?

How do you change who you are and what you are doing?

In 1956, George Miller released a paper titled, "The Magical Number Seven—Plus or Minus Two."

Miller discovered that, depending on a person's mood or mindset, their conscious mind could hold seven plus or minus two bits of information at one time.

For example, if someone is feeling good or optimistic, they can hold a total of nine things in their mind. If they are feeling bad, or they are not interested in something, they can only retain five things in their mind.

In his study, the more a person focused on something they didn't like, the less they were able to think about anything else except those things that they didn't like, or those things that bothered them.

If you concentrate on enough negative thoughts, you become oblivious to any other possibilities.

You become what you think about.

Now combine this with an unconscious mind that is constantly being fed reports of fear or negativity from family members telling you how you are no good, friends telling you that you will never make it, the newspaper and media shouting at you how impossible it is to get ahead.

It is no wonder that all you can find growing in the fertile ground of your life is weeds. You reap a harvest of lack, planted by fear and watered by the voices of negativity.

To change your harvest, you have to reprogram not only what is in your conscious mind, but also what is in your sub-conscious (or unconscious) mind.

If the thoughts planted in your unconscious mind are seeds of doubt and fear, they will grow like weeds and strangle the dreams, goals and possibilities you are trying to focus on.

You will reap a harvest of destruction, not a harvest that leads to prosperity, possibility and a worthwhile future.

Because you become what you think about.

Ever run a mental rabbit trail? You're lying there in bed and everything is fine, then all of a sudden you start to think about your kids. You

    you will never have what you want
    if you don't go after it

    the answer will always be no
    if you don't ask for it

    you will always be in the same place
    if you don't step forward

3 SIMPLE RULES

become convinced that they are going to go out and do something they shouldn't, and if they get caught, they will go to jail. Jail time will lead to gang violence and a vicious prison raping. Upon their release, you are absolutely sure that they will take up drugs to drown out their memories, become a dealer to support their habit, and die in a gun battle with authorities in a South American country.

You get up, race into her room and she is fast asleep in her penguin onesie she got for her 5th birthday...yesterday.

True story. Kids...sigh.

In order to gain success in our lives and maximize our potential, we must control our thinking, because our thinking determines our actions.

Henry Ford said, "Whether you believe you can or whether you believe you can't…you're right."

Here's a head trip—the same opportunity that leads to success can lead to failure.

Why?

Basically, as Henry Ford said, you get what you go for. Our internal responses lead to external behavior. What is in you is going to come out of you at some point in time. More often than not, it is under times of stress or pressure that the "real you" shines.

You cannot just simply tell yourself to change the way you talk or act. You have to change the way you think. This will change your internal responses, which manifest into a different external behavior. In order to gain success in our lives, we must control our thinking.

If you say, "I will always be fat," you will be. If you say, "I will always be poor," you will be.

IN ORDER TO GAIN SUCCESS IN OUR LIVES, WE MUST CONTROL OUR THINKING.

If you say, "We could never afford a house like that," you're absolutely right, you never will.

Come on, say it out loud and scare the cat: YOU BECOME WHAT YOU THINK ABOUT.

By now, you should be realizing that the real question is: "How do I think differently in order to become all I can become?" Notice I said all that YOU can be, not all that your neighbor is, not someone nicer than your ex-wife says you are. I mean YOU.

I do not subscribe to the thought that you can be "everything and anything you want to be." It's just not logical. We all desire to improve ourselves, but this desire to self-improvement can actually be self-destructive if we do not take into account our personality, our genetic make up, our personal disposition and our education.

I am not trying to undermine all that I have just said. I am trying to be realistic and balanced. I've been in those meetings where they tell you, "If you can imagine it and you confess it, the Universe will bring it to you." Rubbish. I am still waiting on my unicorn.

Disappointment arises out of unmet expectations. Common sense plays a part in all successful life and business planning. For example, if you don't have your high school diploma, don't start by declaring you want to be a brain surgeon by the end of the year. Start first by setting the improvement goal of a Bachelor in Something Useful For A Brain Surgeon.

If you have no sense of pitch or a singing voice, don't sign up for American Idol—no really please don't, I spend way too much time watching those people on Youtube when I should be working… yes, you do sound as bad as William Hung.

When you begin to understand that self-knowledge is the beginning of self-correction and self-development, you have come to a place of being able to harness your full potential. You are no longer looking outside of yourself for the milestones of your growth, but internally to what you really do desire. I talk about this extensively in my book, "Living From The Inside Out."

You have to expel your very natural self-doubt, and start to replace it with the seemingly impossible self-confidence built on a solid foundation of realistic expectations. The secret to doing this is to fill your mind with thoughts of confidence, security and hope. Now don't go and get all, "I've tried this stuff and it doesn't work." I am going to give you some "how to do's" to your "what to do's" in the coming pages.

But just for now, imagine this:

Imagine training your mind to replace the old

and negative thoughts you have about yourself with the new and positive thoughts you want to have. How much more fulfilled, productive, energized and passionate would you be about what you do on a daily basis?

Imagine that if you discipline your time use and make a realistic plan, you could double your effectiveness in say, 3 months. (It's a good start.) You could accomplish twice as much in the same amount of time. You could possibly double the speed at which you accomplish your objectives. This might lead to you cutting in half the time it takes you to achieve your dreams and goals and become the brain surgeon you want to be.

I know, I know...sounds like an infomercial.

But really is it?

We all give a nod to the old saying, "Don't work harder, work smarter."

If that is something we all agree with, then isn't the issue really how do we actually work smarter?

In order to work smarter, you have to start THINKING smarter.

THE ROLE OF THE UNCONSCIOUS MIND

George Miller proved that this was true. Just by concentrating on the positive, you almost double your capacity to achieve.

What is the difference between what some people refer to as the "unconscious" and "subconscious" mind?

Although it is used often, the "subconscious" is not actually a proper psychological term.

There are three types of consciousness:

- Conscious
- Preconscious
- Unconscious (This is what most people are referring to when they say "subconscious").

The conscious is what you perceive, your controlled thought.

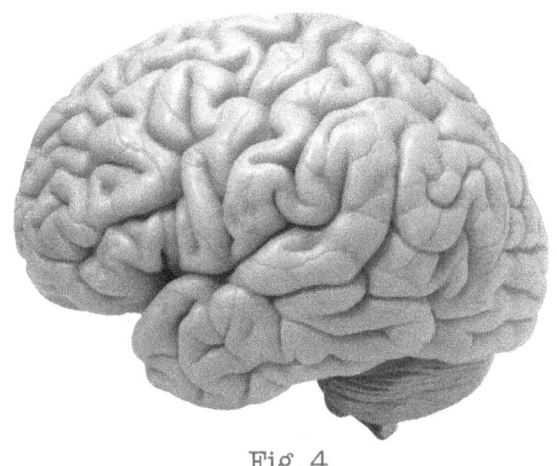

Fig. 4

The preconscious is what you can easily focus on and bring up quickly from memory.

The unconscious mind is what is going on "underneath the surface," without us being consciously aware.

GOOD AIR IN, BAD AIR OUT

Have you ever noticed that you don't have to think about breathing?

Your body's simple request for more oxygen generates an automatic response.

It is an unconscious activity, or rather, an activity that you are not consciously aware of.

Not only does the unconscious mind control the running of our bodies, it can also have a tremendous impact on the results we get in every aspect of our conscious life.

If you have set yourself a conscious goal and yet your unconscious mind, your inner thoughts, and your inner desire have another agenda, you will have inner tension. Your physical, mental and spiritual resources will not be focused to achieve the same results.

YOU MUST GET YOUR UNCONSCIOUS MIND ON BOARD AND WORKING WITH YOU, NOT AGAINST YOU.

To achieve the greatest success, we must endeavor to align both our conscience and our unconscious minds with our goals.

The conscious and unconscious minds excel at different things. The conscious mind is like the top 10% of an iceberg; the subconscious is the other 90%.

One of the roles of the unconscious mind is to preserve and manage memories. It holds some, it suppresses some and others it keeps constantly circling through your conscious mind.

Ready and Burton in their book on neuro-

Fig. 5

linguistic programing suggest that the unconscious mind cannot process negatives. It can only process everything as a positive or an active emotion.

Therefore if you say to yourself, "I don't want to be bitter or angry," it doesn't register the "don't." The unconscious mind interprets this statement or thought as, "I want to be bitter and angry."

It does not hear the negative statement, only the positive action.

If you say, "I don't want to be poor," it hears, "I want to be poor." If you say, "I don't want to be sick," it hears, "I want to be sick."

I know, total head trip.

It can be really distressing when you first find out about it, but you can actually turn this quirk into a powerful ally by reprogramming how you think about yourself, how you talk about yourself, and how you talk to others.

Don't try to program your mind with feelings, it just won't work. Don't try and feeeeel good about work. Don't try and feeeeel successful. Don't try and feeeeel good about yourself or your future, or the cowboys ever winning another superbowl. (BRING ON THE HATE MAIL BIG BOY)! Rather, work with that weird little quirk of your subconscious we just discussed and start first to develop positive statements of fact about yourself, your life and your future. You will also have to work on your heart response, we talk about that a little later.

For example:

- I want to be happy.
- I am a peaceful person.
- I want to be prosperous.
- I am healthy.
- I am a good husband/wife.

- I am a good friend.
- I am a good parent.

Your unconscious mind is a lean, mean, learning machine; but it needs direction. The beautiful thing is that it wants to learn and it is programmable.

Your unconscious mind can be the greatest aid to inner peace and motivation when harnessed, but you have to keep it fed with possibilities and the right resources. As I have said before, you have to sow the right seed into the the fertile ground of your mind.

You must get your unconscious mind on board and working with you, not against you. Once you do, you can and will achieve more in life. Why? Because every waking or sleeping moment of the day you will be focused on and contemplating the goals that you have set for yourself and not even "thinking" about it.

THE ISSUE OF SELF SABOTAGE

Every time that I encounter people who are inwardly afraid, who shrink away from life, its challenges and possibilities—they all seem to suffer deep down from a sense of inadequacy, insecurity and lack of confidence.

They strike me as if they are beset by vague

and sinister fears that something will not work out for them, that something is wrong, or is just about to go wrong, or has gone wrong and they haven't received the letter about it yet.

It's like deep down within themselves, they mistrust and doubt their ability to grasp and fulfill opportunities that are presented to them.

"I knew this would never work out."

"Things like this always happen to me."

Remember, our unconscious does not know what is a positive or negative fact.

Self-sabotage is one of the symptoms that people experience when their unconscious mind is in conflict with their conscious mind.

How do we self-sabotage? We listen to our unconscious mind.

Your unconscious mind wants to bring back memories and snapshots of the past to preserve itself and protect you from angst and emotional pain that you have suffered. It reminds you of what happened last time you tried and failed or stumbled. How much it hurt. How badly you were embarrassed. How everyone is laughing at that stupid youtube video of you on the treadmill at the gym three years ago. A negative unconscious mind is like an obnoxious Super Villain.

Fig. 6

When we give in to replaying past experiences, we go into survival mode. We start preparing for failure, heartache and disappointment. The super villain sees itself as a super hero that is trying to cocoon us from experiences that have previously been painful.

When you allow the negative emotion and or negative memory to dominate your mind, you are literally reliving your past, one bitter and hurtful memory at a time.

The only way around this is to program yourself with a positive memory. For example ask yourself, "What did I learn from that experience?" Or remember the feeling of great joy you had when you finally got out of that relationship or away from the co-worker from hell. Now, every time the memory and negative emotion pops into your head (for me that always seems to be between 2:30 am and 3 am), you have something very concrete to start your reprogramming with.

Sounds too easy to be true? It is easy and it is true—the hard part is to remember to do it and not lie there in cold sweats. This technique is the one I used over and over again since the 2008 implosion. I replaced memories of sexual abuse with feelings of victory and survival at having "made it out alive" from my childhood.

Another area I really struggled with was an inferiority complex. I grew up being told day after day that I was "Captain Concrete—thick and dense." I often heard, "How come you're not smart like your sister? You'll never amount to anything, you're too stupid."

These all hurt, and to be honest, they still do.

When the feeling of not being smart enough to be loved, or not being good enough to be cared for come back, I sit down and remind myself what it felt like to graduate school. I remember what it felt like to receive my postgraduate degrees.

The degree is not what I focus on, but the feeling of knowing I'm not as stupid as I was told.

The greatest secret for eliminating the inferiority complex, which is another term for deep and profound self-doubt, is to fill your mind to overflowing with a belief in yourself and a belief in your future. I am not talking about

flights of fancy, I am talking about focusing on your passions, your dreams, your vision for your life and your future.

Each day of our lives we are building up feelings of insecurity or feelings of security based upon what we are thinking about.

THE POWER OF REMEMBER WHEN

Some exercises that people have found helpful in building a bank of positive images is to recall what it felt like to win at different times in their lives, or to remember a time when they experienced success.

EACH DAY OF OUR LIVES WE ARE BUILDING UP FEELINGS OF INSECURITY OR SECURITY BASED ON WHAT WE THINK ABOUT.

You see, your heart and mind don't work on a timeline. They don't keep a chronological memory, and you can use that to your advantage. The feeling of winning or being joyful or being at peace can be recalled and meditated upon, and your heart and your mind think that it is happening in the present. Your body will release all the hormones that bring the comfort and pleasure with those memories.

(Did he just say heart? Really? Is this guy

stupid or what?! Hearts don't have memories. (Just wait 2 more pages)).

Take those thoughts and play those thoughts over and over again, consciously dwell on them. To dwell is to think about something for a considerable length of time, to meditate on it, and to consider it deeply. This process replaces negative self-talk or emotions with positive memories.

Another tool that people have found helpful is to create a victory journal. In this journal they take paper clippings, photos, key events, goals and past achievements and scrapbook all that stuff together. They build their stories and keep a journal of their journey of wins along they way as they head towards wholeness and change.

Fig. 7

Those who keep these journals tell me that they have found it helpful to stop self-doubt and break the cycle of self-sabotage by harnessing the power of a renewed unconscious mind.

Journaling is something that you can start now with past victories, and keep adding new stories of wholeness and change as you go.

Remember, the most dangerous thing in the world is an idea, especially a positive one. It is dangerous to your sense of failure, to your loneliness, to your lack of fulfillment and lack of excitement with your life.

In my house each year we do a Vision Board. We stick together pictures that represent all the things we are believing to happen for the year ahead, and we hang it somewhere were we can see it each day. The pictures mean nothing to anyone but us. It's not a show piece, it's a focus piece. We keep the vision of the life we want to build before us on a daily basis.

For me this is very important. I have to keep reminding myself of where I've come from and where I want to go to keep from sliding back into the sticky tar pit of my past and my mind.

EVERYTHING STARTS AS A THOUGHT

Everything starts as a thought. Everything.

Everything we desire, or we participate in, starts as a thought, an idea, or a suggestion.

Yet most people give very little regard to their thinking.

Thoughts are things. They are tangible. They are real.

Your thoughts are you, and you are your thoughts.

The thoughts you had yesterday constructed the decisions you made that led you to the place you are now.

King Solomon wrote, "As a man thinks in His heart so is he."

The Hebrew word for heart means "living being."

A study was published in the Spring 2002 issue of the Journal of Near-Death Studies entitled, "Changes in Heart Transplant Recipients That Parallel the Personalities of Their Donors."

The study consisted of open-ended interviews with ten heart or heart-lung transplant recipients, their families or friends, and the donor's families or friends. The researchers reported striking parallels in each of the cases.

What they discovered was that the heart has a system of neurons, or a neurological system similar to that of the brain. The way the heart processes information was the same as the brain. The heart has something called a cellular memory.

The conclusion of the study was that as the brain processes information by taking facts and coming to some rationalization as a result of those facts, the heart also arrives at conclusions, not based on facts, but upon what it interprets and feels as a result of an incident or experience.

They concluded that the heart records information much like the brain, but the heart attaches an emotion to every piece of information that it records.

Dr. Paul Pearsall was one doctor involved in this research, and he recorded some of his findings and case studies in a book entitled, "The Heart's Code."

Paul Oldam, a lawyer from Milwaukee, received the heart of a fourteen year-old boy, and inherited the young man's craving for Snickers, a candy he had never liked before.

A man of twenty-five received a woman's heart and, to his girlfriend's delight, developed a desire to go shopping.

A fifty-two year-old male received the heart from a seventeen year-old boy who was killed by a hit-and-run driver. Before the transplant, he loved quiet classical music. After the transplant, his musical taste radically changed, and he now thoroughly enjoys loud rock music.

Then there is the case of Claire Sylvia, who Kate Linton mentions in her paper, "Knowing By Heart."

On May 29, 1988, a woman named Claire Sylvia received the heart of an eighteen year-old male who had been killed in a motorcycle accident. Soon after the operation, Sylvia noticed some distinct changes in her attitudes, habits, and tastes. She found herself acting in a more masculine manner, strutting down the street (which, being a dancer, was a bit awkward for her to explain). She began craving foods such as green peppers and beer, things she had always disliked before.

Sylvia even began having recurring dreams about a mystery man named Tim L., who she had a feeling was her donor. As it turns out, he was. Upon meeting the "family of her heart," as she put it, Sylvia discovered that her donor's name was, in fact, Tim L., and that all the changes she had been experiencing in her attitudes, tastes, and habits closely mirrored that of Tim's.

People thought the cases were just coincidence; many medical professionals were skeptical. Then came one case they could not deny.

There was an eight year-old girl in the Northwest of the U.S.A. who received a heart transplant from another young girl who had been ten years of age and the victim of murder.

The little girl who received the successful heart transplant began to have dreams that a man was chasing her. She believed that these dreams were of the man who had murdered her donor. Over time, the dreams that started out vague became clearer and clearer. It got to the point where these were no longer dreams, but terrifying nightmares. Her parents were very concerned because she couldn't sleep at night. They took her to a psychologist, who, after several sessions, declared that she "could not deny the reality of what the child was telling her."

There came a point where the little girl started to describe things like the setting of house and its contents. She described everything—right down to the individual who was chasing her in the dreams. She described the place, the time, the clothes and even the weapon used to kill her donor.

Her parents and psychologist got the police involved.

Paul Pearsall relates the story in his book. "The police sketch artist came in and they had the little girl describe everything that she was going through and everything that she saw. They actually were able to get a sketch of

a man, a house and the interior of the house. This led police to the killer, who happened to be a neighbor of the little girl, the heart donor, who had been killed. They found evidence in the house that convicted, by trial and jury, the man of this murder."

BESIDES FREAKING ME OUT, HOW DOES IT APPLY TO ME?

When you allow thoughts of fear, thoughts of stress, thoughts of anxiety to take root in your heart and you start to dwell on them, you allow these fears to become a substance.

Your heart has a memory. It remembers emotion and it cannot tell which memory is real and which is not—that's why horror movies work.

You're sitting there, with popcorn in a movie theater. The scariest thing there is the amount of cholesterol in the artificial butter. Some hand puppet comes to life, starts killing people and you jump so high, popcorn covers everyone around you. None of it was real, (except your wife dropping her soda in your lap and everyone thinking you peed yourself), but your heart and your mind cannot tell the difference between a real scare and an artificial one.

As you think in your head and feel in your heart, so you are. Everything starts as a thought, becomes a desire, then moves to a vision and is out-worked in action.

As negative desires become negative things, so can positive desires become positive things. You have to take control of your mind, your desires and emotions to take control of your life.

Your subconscious doesn't know the difference between visions of greatness or the longings of a loser. It just knows that you spend the majority of your time thinking about a particular thing in a particular way. It does not attach moral or ethical value to those things—we do.

WHAT YOU SAY, YOU MEAN

Have you ever caught yourself saying something hurtful, and then following it up by saying that you were only joking? If you are truly honest, you know you were not!

That was really how you felt, or what you meant to say, harmful and hurtful though it was.

If you get into a habit of listening to yourself speak and noticing the words that you say, you will be able to identify the areas that you need to develop and discipline in your life.

Your words create your world.

"Optimist: Someone who figures that taking a step backward after taking a step forward is not a disaster, it's a cha-cha."
—Robert Brault

A thought becomes a desire, which becomes a vision that is articulated and is then pursued as a goal.

You pursue that thing which is your focus, and your focus becomes your reality. If you truly want to change your life, if you truly want to change your outcome, do not try and start with a change in behavior.

Start with a change in your thought life.

As a result, your thoughts will become a desire that will move to a vision.

You will then find yourself starting to speak about them to yourself and others.

Ultimately, you will start to focus on them, and

what used to be a future dream will become a passionate pursuit, then a present reality. It is not namby-pamby, new age nonsense as many detractors will say. It is a spiritual truth with scientific proof.

CHAPTER 4
WHAT IS SUCCESS?

"The race is not to the swift or the strong, but time and chance are given to us all."

—King Solomon

LUCK vs. OPPORTUNITY

King Solomon said, "The race is not to the swift or the strong, but time and chance are given to us all."

In other words, everyone gets a shot at the prize. We may not all have the same talent, but we all have time, and we all have a chance. The determining factor is whether or not we make the most of our opportunities, and whether or not we are prepared for our opportunities when they present themselves.

I have heard people say things like, "He got a lucky break," or, "If I had her luck I could be successful," or, "She is lucky. Look at the family she came from."

In Roman mythology, Fortuna was the goddess of fortune or luck. This veiled and blind daughter of Jupiter had a great number of shrines erected in her honor, and people would make sacrifices on her altar in the hope that they would be granted favorable fortune or good luck. When fortune and luck were not bestowed, the goddess was said to be fickle and temperamental.

I do not believe in luck.

Luck is the excuse we use when we don't want to

take responsibility for outcomes we don't like.

What others ascribe to luck, I attribute to successful people meeting opportunity with preparedness.

What if we think of success altogether differently? What if it's not at the pinnacle, one-time, mountaintop destination? What if success lies in the day in, day out series of decisions that make us who we are?

Success, then, is not a thing we do or a location we arrive at, but a journey we are making, a path that we are on. I have come to define success for myself as the passionate and active pursuit of a worthwhile goal.

Along that track toward that goal, as we prepare for our passion, as we get ready for our goal, as we set our hearts and minds on what is ahead, we are presented with opportunities. And we take them. We are ready for them.

These opportunities become ours and they launch us up to the next thing that we are aiming for.

SUCCESS IS THE PASSIONATE AND ACTIVE PURSUIT OF A WORTHWHILE GOAL.

A fickle Roman goddess has nothing to do with it.

Luck didn't get you out of bed at six a.m. to study. Luck doesn't take you out the door when you aren't feeling your best. Luck doesn't make you walk forty-five minutes through the rain when your car broke down on the way to meet a client.

Passion does. Persistence does. Preparation does.

So when someone sees your passion, they see your commitment, they see your dedication, they give you an opportunity.

And you are prepared for it.

That is discipline. That is hard work. That is a belief in what you are called to do.

That is not luck; that is the passionate pursuit of a worthwhile goal.

I am an amateur body builder, and it takes years to prepare for a competition. When you step out on that stage painted orange and in a swim suit the size of a handkerchief, luck has nothing to do with it.

A lazy person, if they have not worked their buns off (get it? BUNS off), can step out onto that stage with the greatest genes, but if they didn't

put the work in, they will be fat, bloated and embarrassed—as well as orange in swimmers the size of a handkerchief.

THE ROLE OF CHARACTER

I believe the biggest difference between making the most of an opportunity and missing an opportunity is our character.

Talents are what you are born with. Character is something we all have an opportunity to develop. Character is not genetically inherited. It is developed by a series of decisions.

William Jennings Bryan said, "Destiny is no matter of chance. It is a matter of choice. It is not a thing to be waited for. It is a thing to be achieved."

Your destiny is not based upon the situation of your birth, but upon the decisions you make and the company you keep.

What you have set before you every day is the same as every other person on the planet. You have an opportunity—an opportunity to find a reason, or an opportunity to make an excuse:

- A reason to be great or an excuse to be small.

- A reason to succeed or an excuse for your failure.

- A reason to prosper or someone to blame for your lack.

- A reason to get out of bed or an excuse to sleep in.

- A reason to make the call or an excuse not to.

George Washington said, "It is better to offer no

excuse than a bad one." Most people's excuses are little more than justification for their failures.

Their failure to be on time. Their failure to study. Their failure to exercise. Their failure to attend. Their failure to prepare. Their failure to be ready.

We can all respect the person who says, "I don't want to do that," or even, "I just couldn't be bothered doing that." But we all find it difficult to listen to someone go down the list of "would have, could have, should have."

If I had allowed my past to be an excuse, it would have been terminal. I didn't, and you don't have to either.

CHAPTER 5
THE POWER OF PERSISTENCE

"The secret to success is constancy to purpose."

—Benjamin Disraeli

TUCK YOUR CHIN
AND THROW PUNCHES

SUCCESS ARISES FROM ADVERSITY

Success in life arises out of adversity. Success in business is born out of failure.

Glenn Cunningham was only seven years old when a classroom stove exploded, injuring him and killing his brother. Glenn's legs were severely burned, and the doctors recommended amputation because they doubted that he would ever walk again.

Cunningham's mother determined that her son would improve and refused to allow the amputation. Sure enough, with the help of his mother, Cunningham learned to walk again. (Got to love it when someone sees YOU, and not what you can't DO.)

Cunningham was not satisfied with simply walking, he wanted to run.

By the time he was twelve, he was not only running, he was running faster than everyone else at his school.

His deeply scarred legs prevented him from running smoothly or efficiently, but he made up for his ungainly stride with endurance and strength. Before competing in races, Cunningham had to spend a lot of time massaging his legs and doing warm-up exercises.

When he was thirteen years old, Cunningham

won his first mile-long race. Although he participated in many other sports, he excelled at running.

He set records as a University of Kansas student. He competed twice in the fifteen hundred meter event at the Olympics. He came in fourth in 1932 and won a silver medal in 1936. Cunningham was elected to the U.S. National Track and Field Hall of Fame and named the most outstanding track athlete to compete at Madison Square Garden during its first one hundred years.

Thomas J. Watson said, "If you stand up and be counted, from time to time you may get yourself knocked down. But remember this: a man flattened by an opponent can get up again. A man flattened by conformity stays down for good."

Benjamin Disraeli said, "The secret to success is constancy to purpose."

Most of us were never made aware of the simple truth that failure is a choice, just as success is a matter of choice.

A champion is not someone who never fails, just someone who never quits.

Failure is not the result of education, lack of talent, money or a matter of where and when you where born. Failure is simply the refusal to set worthwhile goals and work consistently and persistently towards them. Failure is simply the refusal to get up one more time.

To succeed and to achieve you are going to constantly find yourself going beyond the map of your normal experience.

Any time you are breaking new ground, any time you are taking a risk, any time you are doing something for the first time, there is always the possibility of failure. In fact, if you're honest, you are guaranteed a degree of failure because if success were easy, everyone would be successful.

When reaching for any dream, any goal, any objective, short term or long term, you either succeed or you don't. The more distant your objective, the more times you can expect to fall short of your expectations and fall flat on your face.

A course correction is not a course deviation. It is just that; a correction. Not a failure, a correction. When sailing, you know your destination. The goal doesn't change, but you are having to constantly monitor factors from a variety of sources such as wind shifts and sea currents. You are constantly making small corrections, or sometimes even large changes to meet the end goal. It is simply a realignment of your current position with your proposed end goal.

Remember the goal is the goal. Sailing in a straight line was never the goal—getting to have a picnic on the deserted island with your wife (and getting up to no good) was always the goal.

I have defined success for you as the passionate and active pursuit of a worthwhile goal.

Underline the word passionate.

Passionate: compelled, intense, marked by strong feeling. If your goal is not something that moves you or drives you, then it is not something that will keep you going when the going gets tough—and friend, it WILL get tough.

The greatest lesson I learned about achieving what seemed like an impossible goal in the midst of overwhelming obstacles was to just keep turning up.

I see people all the time make that same simple, yet most profound choice to grow and develop in the midst of horrendous personal tragedy and difficulty.

They felt depressed. But they just kept turning up.

They were financially destitute. But they just kept turning up.

They had cancer. But they just kept turning up.

They had marriage problems. But they just kept turning up.

Their kids were in jail. But they just kept turning up.

Abraham Lincoln said, "My concern is not whether you have failed, but whether you are content with your failure."

Abraham Lincoln experienced many failures during his lifetime, both before and during his political career. In 1831, he opened his first business, a dry goods store, which later went out of business.

In 1832, he entered the Black Hawk War with the rank of captain, but left three months later as a private without ever seeing battle. He also lost an election for the state legislature and was defeated as elector.

He then purchased another store in a different location, but it also closed, leaving Lincoln in considerable debt. His brief stint as postmaster produced the worst efficiency record in the county.

In 1834, Lincoln ran for the Illinois House of Representatives and won, but later lost his bid to serve as Speaker of the House.

In 1835, his girlfriend died.

The following year, Lincoln had a nervous breakdown. In 1837, he fell in love again, but the woman turned down his proposal.

In 1843, Lincoln lost an election for the U.S. Congress, although he won the next time he ran, he later failed to win reelection.

In 1854, he was elected to the Illinois legislature, but he declined the seat in order to run for the U.S. Senate, only to lose that election.

In 1856, he ran for vice president and lost.

Two years later, he ran for the U.S. Senate again, and lost again.

In 1860, he ran for President of the United States and won with 40 percent of the popular vote, although he had 60 percent of the electoral votes.

In 1863, he signed the Emancipation Proclamation. Defeat is a decision. Lincoln was not defeated because he refused to quit. He kept turning up.

I honestly believe that success is a decision. It is a decision that the goal you are seeking is worth giving everything to and that nothing will stand in your way.

Most people never get anywhere or achieve anything because they don't know where they are going or what they want to do when they get there.

You may die in the pursuit of your goal; you may die not having achieved it. That being said, you did not die a failure. Remember, we defined success as the passionate pursuit of a worthwhile goal.

A fruitful and successful life is found in the persistent and dogged pursuit of one dream after another. No one dream should ever satisfy you, no one goal should ever be enough. The moment you arrive where you think you are supposed to be going is the moment you set your sight on new aspects of your vision and purpose.

That is why it is the pursuit of the goal—the dream with passion and determination—that is the measure of our success, not the obtaining of a benchmark, not buying a thing or doing an activity.

Most people don't agree with this, and that's all right. I don't want to be most people. Some say defeat is not a decision, bad things just happen to them all the time.

Well I agree with them. Bad things do happen all the time, not only to them, but to everyone.

But I say they decided to sit out this round. I say they made a decision to quit.

If success and perseverance are decisions, then so is defeat.

Think it through, you know this is correct. You know this is true and not just self-help guru speak.

If success were environmental, then only some would reach their goals in life. If perseverance were based on a personality type, then only certain types of people would succeed.

Again: Success is a decision. Perseverance is a decision.

Therefore, using the same logic, defeat is a

decision. If you expect failure, you will get failure.

But if you expect to succeed, you will succeed. Why? Because you won't stop this side of glory till you do. If it comes down to it, you will die trying with a smile. Why? Because you were passionately pursuing your goal. You were successful.

IF SUCCESS AND PERSEVERANCE ARE DECISIONS, THEN SO IS DEFEAT.

George Lorimer said, "Because a fellow has failed once or twice, or a dozen times, you don't want to set him down as a failure till he's dead or loses his courage—and that's the same thing."

Milton Hershey opened his first candy store in Pennsylvania in 1876 at the age of nineteen. For six years, he worked around the clock manufacturing the candy at night and selling it during the day. After he collapsed from exhaustion, Hershey closed the business and moved to Denver to work for another candy company.

After gaining some experience, he moved to Chicago and tried to run his own business again, but it failed as well.

He opened yet another company in New York

City, only to fail again.

Finally, Hershey moved back to Lancaster Pennsylvania and scraped together enough money, since no one would lend him any after so many failures, to start the Lancaster Caramel Company.

Despite his failures, he had managed to perfect a recipe for caramels that used fresh milk, making them much creamier than the standard fare.

This new recipe proved to be the key to his success. Sales improved, enabling him to procure a loan and expand the business.

In 1900, Hershey sold his caramel company for $1 million and focused entirely on chocolate. In just a few years, his chocolate business was worth more than $20 million. His chocolate was so popular that the town where Hershey began his company, Derry Church Pennsylvania, changed its name to Hershey, and is often called Chocolate Town U.S.A.

AN EXERCISE IN PERSISTENCE

Are you still not sure if this will work?

Are you still throwing down the B.S. flag and calling it all "self-help mumbo jumbo?"

Let's take an easily recognizable and common goal that people often set themselves: getting into better physical condition.

You decide one day to get in shape. Your goals are to become physically fit, lose some weight, and improve the quality of your life.

Remember this: your goal has three very specific and personal aspects to it.

1. become physically fit

2. lose some weight

3. improve the quality of your life

You decide that you will use the vehicle of training for a marathon to motivate yourself to reach your goal. You give yourself 6 months to get into not-collapsing-and-dying-on-camera shape. You find a date for a marathon, you come up with a schedule, and you set your sights on the finish line.

In the process of training, you sprain your ankle so badly that the doctor says you can't run for another six weeks. There is just no way that you can be fit enough to run a marathon.

You get depressed. Discouraged. You start to slip back into old routines and habits. But then you catch yourself on the couch with a dozen donuts, and you remember what the original

Fig. 8

goals were.

Your goal wasn't to run a marathon. Your goal was to become physically fit, to lose some weight and to enjoy a better quality of life.

You don't throw your hands in the air and shake your fists at God and decide that the universe is against you, you just change tactics. You make a course correction.

You can't run, but you can swim. You decide to get together with a bunch of mates and enter a group triathlon, with you handling the swim leg.

The goal hasn't changed. The strategy may have, but not the goal—you are back on the path to success.

Anyone can keep going when the going is good. You may say, "You don't know me. You don't know how hard I have it. Nobody is as low as I am."

Well, that may be true, but think of it this way: you are in the best position of your life. Every way is up for you. Everything is forward.

At probably the lowest point in my life a member of the Back Deck Crew (you'll learn more about them later) said, "John, you're in a hole, but for some reason you just keep digging. I would suggest that before you try to start climbing out, you throw the bloody shovel out so you're not tempted to dig any deeper."

I looked at this 5'5"-5'6" dynamo of a woman— she and her husband are my closest friends— and I laughed. She was so right. (Her husband suggested that I dig foot holds first. He is in marketing, she's an engineer...it got fun after that).

When faced with failure, forward is your only choice. You cannot embrace the future when you are anchored to the past.

Your past will either define you for the rest of your life, or refine you and sharpen you for your future. It will either be a quagmire that will drag you down, or a foundation upon which you will build tomorrow.

YOU NEED TO INVEST IN A DAILY PROGRAM OF REWRITING YOUR INNER SCRIPT.

To get to where you want to go, you must first firmly plant your feet on the ground where you are and not be moved by where you have been.

When faced with defeat or difficult situations, the only person you have control over is you, and the only time you have is now.

In the purest sense, neither I nor anyone else can help you succeed, but neither can we make you fail.

No one has the power to make you feel like a failure, unless you give it to them.

You can either react or respond to your past and to others' comments. You have no power to change your past physically or emotionally, however you do have power to change your response to the past in the present and in the future.

Don't let your unconscious mind rule your conscious world. Your unconscious is running off the years of negative programming you have given it. It has years of bad words and negativity invested into it.

You need to invest in a daily program of

rewriting your inner script.

JANE AUSTIN BEFORE SHE SLAYED ZOMBIES

Jane Austen said, "There will be little rubs and disappointments everywhere, and we are all apt to expect too much; but then, if one scheme of happiness fails, human nature turns to another; if the first calculation is wrong, we make a second better."

Jane Austen was extremely shy. To prevent people from noticing what she was doing, she wrote her first novel on scraps of paper that she would tuck away under her desk blotter when anyone entered her room.

At some point, she collected the scraps and compiled them into a complete book titled, "First Impressions."

In 1797, she gathered up the courage to show the novel to her father. He liked it so much that he queried a publisher to see if the firm would be interested in it.

The publisher rejected it by return of post. Discouraged, Austen shelved First Impressions, and focused her attention on a second novel, "Susan." Six years later, in 1803, Austen managed to get a publisher interested enough

to buy the book, but the firm never published it.

After these two major setbacks, Austen went to work on a new novel.

It took her eight years before she dared to send it to a publisher. This time, a publisher purchased it and issued the book under the title, "Sense and Sensibility."

It was a huge success, and the first edition sold out within a year. The success of the novel encouraged Austen to revise her original novel, "First Impressions." It was published two years later under a new title, "Pride and Prejudice."

Today, "Pride and Prejudice" is Austen's most famous work, and placed second in a 2003 BBC poll as the best-loved book in the United Kingdom. It has been adapted for television, stage, and motion pictures, and has inspired numerous other works, including the best-selling novel by Helen Fielding, "Bridget Jones's Diary," and my favorite date night film, "Pride and Prejudice and Zombies."

8 THINGS THAT HELPED ME LEARN TO PERSEVERE

So when faced with an obstacle, something that is standing in your way, something that is blocking your path to success, how do you surmount it?

First try and go around it. If you can't go around it, try and get under it. If that doesn't work, try over the top. And if still it is there, walk right through it.

Whatever it is, don't allow it to stop you.

When faced with what seems like insurmountable odds, you don't need a miracle, you need to <u>become</u> the miracle. Becoming the miracle means turning up, refusing to quit, persevering.

I would like to give you eight keys to help you develop perseverance.

1. Have a definite purpose.

It is no good saying, "I will persevere, I will persevere." You are going to persevere at what?

For what reason? At what price? What is your ultimate goal? What is your ultimate aim?

You need to have a strong motivation in order to rise above, go around, or drive straight through the difficulties and challenges that will try and stop you.

Wanting to be "successful" is not enough. What is it you want to be successful at? Why do you want to be successful? What will be the result, and who will be touched and benefit from you fulfilling what you feel you are called to do?

You must be able to answer these questions, or you don't have a vision for your life, you just have a dream. I also talk about this in "Think Big: Living from the Inside Out."

2. Have desire.

You have to really want it. You must count the cost before you ever set out on the journey. You have to be aware that anything of any value is going to be hard to achieve.

Sit down, write it out, look at the pain as well as the prize, and make the conscious decision that regardless of what anybody else says, what anybody else does, you are prepared to give it everything you've got. Decide that you are not, under any circumstances, giving up.

3. Be self-reliant.

There will come a time, before you see success, before you can even see your goal in sight, that you will have to do it all, be it all, believe it all and fight for it all, all by yourself.

You have to develop an inner resilience that will carry you through regardless of what others say or think about you.

That doesn't stop you from asking for help or looking for resources. But if people don't want to help or if they can't help, you must accept that your life is YOUR responsibility.

You are running at YOUR definition of success—this is your "Why"—and no one else can do that for you.

4. Have a clear plan.

Most people do not think through the plan for their success. The truth is most people don't think! They never stop and write out what they believe in and what they are going to achieve. They never stop and ask the next logical question, "How? How is this going to happen? What do I need to do in order to achieve this?"

Most people are waiting for something called luck to turn up. As I said earlier, I don't believe in luck. Making a plan is essential to being prepared, so you can take that opportunity when it presents itself.

5. Acquire knowledge.

You cannot make informed decisions or accurate assessments of what you need to do without the appropriate information.

Knowing that your plans are based upon fact, instead of fantasy, encourages persistence and perseverance. Guessing instead of knowing destroys it.

6. Build a B.D.C.

Some people call this a Brains Trust. In my life this is my Back Deck Crew. When new projects need planning, new business plans need to be discussed, or life just walks up behind me one day and starts beating me with a stick…my wife and I get together on the back deck of our friends' place. We sit for an hour or three and over a bottle of wine and whatever leftovers are available. We chat, we laugh, we cry (that's mostly me), we scheme, we think, we argue over the choice of music...and then move on to more important things like world domination.

You must surround yourself with people who are going where you want to go and who believe in what you are doing.

They don't even have to be working in the same field as you. They don't have to know the ins and outs of your field, but they need to have a sense of greatness and bigness on the inside of them and to see it in you.

Who do you have in your life speaking to you about your future?

7. Make success a habit.

Your mind absorbs and grows as a direct result of what you are constantly feeding it. I have come to believe that persistence is a habit that we all can learn.

If you are feeding your mind fear and failure, then it will constantly achieve just that, fear and failure. Don't give in. While you can still breathe, there is still hope and possibility that if you work your plan with passion that this will be the day your opportunity presents itself.

8. If you don't want to live small, don't dream small.

My concern with most of the people I get to know is not that they think too highly of themselves, but rather that they think too small of their future. I am not talking about having an over blown or unrealistic view of yourself. The truth is that you are probably not as good or as bad as you think you are. Somewhere in the middle of Eeyore and Little Miss Sunshine is probably your personal reality.

Today, most people have a challenge with how long it takes to achieve something of value. We are part of the generations that have redefined the dining experience—formerly a leisurely, intimate affair—to one that is prepared to a stopwatch and shoved down your throat in the front seat of a minivan. Anything of any worth takes time and effort.

Do not dream small, but THINK BIG!

This will take time. It will take blood, sweat and tears/beers, but it will all be worth it.

We have a tendency to overestimate what we can achieve in twelve months and underestimate what we can do in ten years.

You have to be in it for the long haul.

CHAPTER 6
SMILE AND ENJOY THE FIRE

"The moment you doubt you can fly, you cease forever to be able to do it."

—J.M. Barrie

It will take everything you've got to become everything that you want. Every ounce of discipline you can muster, every bit of determination to rise again when you fall is required to keep the end goal in sight.

Lack of vision will drain a person of energy and vitality. I have often seen the most talented people become bored, restless and sometimes physically sick because their minds are filled with nothing but petty problems and situations, worry and stress. They don't have anything bigger to live for.

The simple fact is that you don't burn out doing something you love. You don't become bored and restless and fed up if your mind is filled with passion and possibility.

IT WILL TAKE EVERYTHING YOU'VE GOT TO BECOME EVERYTHING YOU WANT.

Most people are holdouts. Be it in the gym, in relationships, or in life, few people leave the field totally spent. Results do not yield themselves to people who refuse to give themselves completely to their passions or dreams.

When I coached boxing, so many people would try and save themselves for the next round. They were pacing themselves.

But what if life doesn't give you a next round? What if this is your one chance and opportunity in life?

SET IT ALIGHT AND WATCH IT BURN

Dylan Thomas, the Welsh poet wrote, "When one burns ones bridges, what a very nice fire it makes."

Burning a bridge was a practice used by great Roman and Greek generals. When they landed on an enemy's beach or crossed a bridge into enemy territory, they would set fire to their boats or burn the bridges behind them.

There was no way for them to retreat. No way for them to go back. No retreat. No surrender.

You should always look closely at your options prior to a major decision, but once you make it, commit to it with faith, belief and a positive mental attitude. And then don't look back.

What I am trying to get you to see is that if there is no way back, then the only way you can go is forward. You need to do this with wisdom and wise council (ie. your B.D.C.), but you have to DO IT.

The only way you are going to be able to face the battles with no option of retreat is by not dwelling on the pain of the moment, but thinking

Fig. 9

on the fruit of the future. Second-guessing is a total waste of time, energy, and life.

SHUT UP, GET UP AND GO AGAIN

David G. Myers, Professor of Psychology at Hope College, says in his book, Pursuit of Happiness, "Without minimizing catastrophe, the consistent and astonishing result is that the worst emotional consequences of bad events are usually temporary."

Myers quotes the life of W. Mitchell as an example:

In 1971, he was horribly burned, nearly killed, and left fingerless from a freak motorcycle accident. Four years later tragedy struck again. This time he was paralyzed from the waist down in a small plane crash. Though terribly disfigured, he chose not to buy the idea that happiness requires handsomeness. "I am in charge of my own spaceship. It is my up, my down. I could choose to see this situation as a setback or a starting point."

Mitchell is a successful investor today, an environmental activist, and a speaker who encourages people to step back from their own misfortunes. Take a wider view and say, "Maybe that isn't such a big thing after all! Before I was paralyzed there were 10,000 things I could do; now there are 9,000. I can either dwell on the 1,000 I've lost or focus on the 9,000 I have left."

LEARN TO BE CONTENT WHILE HUNGERING FOR MORE

Contentment in the life of people who are constantly striving for success seems to be elusive. The more we have, the more we want. External wealth often produces internal craving, and so the cycle repeats itself. Constant craving for "what is not" robs us of the ability to enjoy and celebrate what is and what we have.

Often people think, "If I had respect I would be happy, if I had money I would be happy, if I had power I would be happy."

If you do not know contentment without these, then the realty is that you will not know contentment with them.

Money is a magnifier. It reveals the true nature of a person. If a person was generous before they become wealthy, they will remain that way. If they were mean-spirited and tight-fisted before they acquired money, they will remain that way.

I once heard it said that money, respect, pleasure, and success are merely the chosen roads that travelers hope to use in order reach this destination of inner contentment.

And yet this contentment remains elusive for many.

After his second Wimbledon victory, Boris Becker surprised the world by admitting his great struggle with suicide.

Jack Higgins, the renowned author of "The Eagle Has Landed," has said that the one thing he knows now, at this high point of his career, which he wished he had known as a small boy is this: "When you get to the top, nothing is there."

SATISFACTION ISN'T ABOUT GETTING WHAT YOU WANT, BUT WANTING WHAT YOU HAVE.

Lee Iacocca, chairman of Chrysler said, "Here I am, in the twilight years of my life, still wondering what it's all about. l can tell you this, fame and fortune is for the birds."

He goes on to explain that, for him, it was only family and close friends that brought the contentment that he so deeply desired.

For many, contentment is tied up with what we have and how much we earn, yet study after study reveals that satisfaction isn't about getting what you want, but wanting what you have. (I deal with this in "Think Big: Big Foot, UFOs, Happiness and Other Modern Myths"). Charles Spurgeon suggested that contentment was a flower from heaven that needed to be cultivated.

I want to help you cultivate that contentment by giving you some very practical steps to take.

In the last few pages, I have included a program that I wrote for myself. This was the program that helped me climb out of my pit and to start the journey forward by re-programming my mind and my life. I call it a 21-day, 10 steps program to help you reprogram your life.

The fact that I call it a 21 day program is total rubbish, but if I told you that it's something you're going to have to do for the rest of your life, or if on the contents page you saw, "Never Ending Program to Deal with the Crap in my Brain," you would never buy the book.

If this chapter title was, "Mate, you are going to have to get up every day of your life and make the decision to do it," more than likely you would throw yourself on the floor and start screaming for the "Instant Gratification Nanny" to come and kiss your emotional boo-boo.

So I won't. I'll lie to you instead.

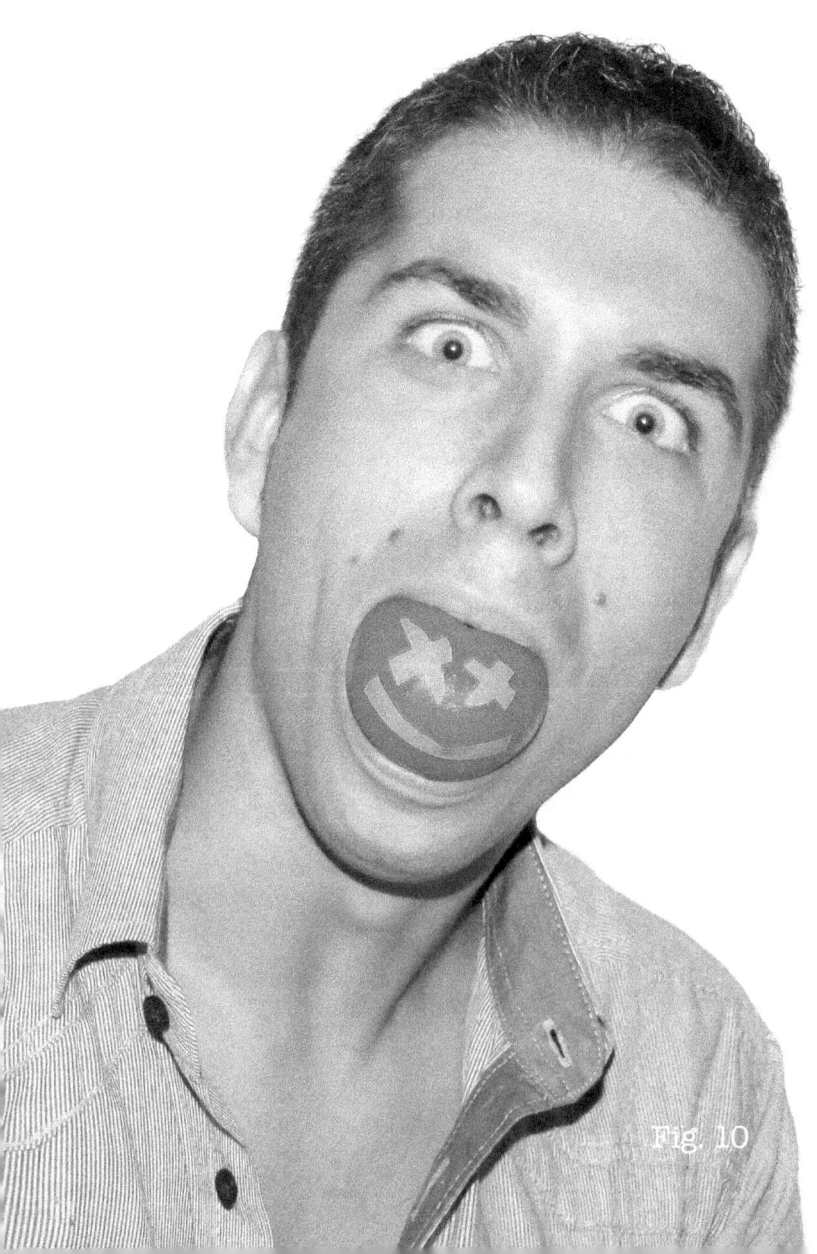

Fig. 10

CHAPTER 7
TIME TO GET REAL

"Would you like an adventure now, or would you like tea first?"

—Peter Pan

21 DAY (Never Ending) DETOX PROGRAM

10 STEPS FOR RE-PROGRAMMING YOUR MENTAL ATTITUDE

WEEK 1

1. Shut up! Refrain and Retrain.

For the next twenty-four hours, you can't say anything negative. For some of you, that means saying nothing at all.

If you do talk, you must deliberately speak positively about everything: Your job, your health, your future, your family, your weight, the country, the economy, everything. Go out of your way to talk optimistically about everything.

This will be difficult for most people, because our habit is to talk pessimistically. You must refrain and start to retrain yourself.

2. Speak out!!

Continue speaking positively 24 hours per day for the rest of the work week.

At the end of five days, you are allowed a two day break. I put these in there for me because at about this point I thought, "Rubbish! What about the REAL WORLD and REAL FEELINGS?"

So I gave myself two "getting back to reality days." In these two days, you can be as "realistic" as you want. You are allowed to drop your guard and not watch your words, but be warned it will come with a price, you will notice a change within you. What was realistic a week ago, you now understand was just negative and depressing—at least that is what happened to me.

I was surprised at how negative everyone around me was, and how negative I was when I just let my mouth and my mind wander. I noticed that I was now hesitant to engage in negative talking and thinking. When I did, I didn't get that little, dirty, satisfied feeling I used to get

Fig. 11

when gossiping or whining about the world and everybody else in it.

3. Make a true assessment of yourself.

Have you ever noticed how easy it is to be "honest" about everyone else? Well this is the opposite. You have to be honest about yourself.

I want you to take stock of how you found last week. Was it easy? Was it tough? What was easy? What was difficult? How did the "Realism Break" make you feel about yourself and your life?

What made you feel hopeless? What filled you with hope?

Now start to make a true and honest assessment of your gifts and passions as you currently see them. Maybe start to craft a passion or vision statement for your life that you can work on over the coming weeks. I didn't know how to do this. What I learned made up the substance of "Think Big: Living from the Inside Out."

This self-examination starts to prepare you to move ahead and start to become the person who will inhabit the life you have always wanted.

WEEK 2

4. Feed Your Mind.

You must feed your mind three times a day as

you would feed your body.

Leaders are Readers.

I could say Leaders are Listeners to Audio Books in the Car on the Way to Work—but it doesn't sound so catchy.

Regardless of what medium you use, make a concentrated effort to expand your mind. Feed yourself with positive, encouraging material. Leadership books, biographies of overcomers, or motivational speeches are good choices. I like to listen to the Bible or an audio book while I go to sleep.

I went as far as limiting my movies and fictional reading to stories of heroes and superheroes. I wanted to make sure that I was doing everything I could to feed my inner being with things to help me get to where I needed/wanted to go.

5. Run away.

Avoid argument, contention, and negativity whenever possible. If you find yourself caught in the middle of contention, find a positive way to excuse yourself from the conversation or situation. Don't feel you have to stand around drowning in someone else's puddle of malcontent.

WEEK 3

6. Friends don't let other friends be losers all their lives.

Get a "let's no longer be losers" partner.

I would encourage you to get someone other than your husband or wife.

Why? Sometimes those closest to us can offer us the greatest resistance when we are trying to change fundamental behaviors. They know us at our worst, and often forget who we can be at our best. If that is not your case, if your spouse is your greatest cheerleader, then go for it.

Once you settle on your "LNLBL" partner, explain to them the program and they will

Knowledge **is** knowing a tomato **is** a fruit.

Wisdom **is** not putting it in a fruit salad.
―Miles Kington

probably want to be all about it.

So...what's the program?

You have to communicate with each other each day for the next seven days. You might send each other an email, make a phone call or meet for coffee. Discuss each others' successes/challenges for the day, and make strategies to handle things better, if necessary, tomorrow.

It is really that simple. On a conscious level you are assessing yourself and identifying good practices that you want to make a daily part of your life. Your partnership may extend beyond the week, but this gives you both an out if it's not working.

7. Make a list of naughty and nice.

Make a list of the people you know, and rate them based on whether they have a positive or negative impact on your life. I am not asking you to judge them, I am asking you to assess the impact they have on your life. This activity is a more long term and deliberate extension of Step 5.

When I knew I had to make a change, I didn't cut off relationships. I simply made the conscious effort to seek out new and more beneficial relationship with people who had a positive and hope-filled view of life. For me it wasn't so much a running away from one group that took place, rather a turning towards a new group to spend my time and emotional capital.

Ask yourself, "Who are the most positive, generous and happy people I know?"

Notice very carefully the words I DID NOT use. I did not use words like rich, powerful, successful or dresses like a pimp, because most of those things are transitory (except maybe dressing like a pimp). Characteristics like happy, nice, generous, content, positive, these are the qualities of the soul of a person, not their external activities.

Make a list of these positive people and deliberately start to cultivate a relationship with them. Get coffee. Buy them lunch. Engage with them.

If you don't know anyone like that, you're screwed.... No you're not, only joking....

No, I am not really. You're toast, you must be horrible.

I just thought I would do that in case your self-loathing and pity party kicked in. Get over your bad self, get out of your cubicle, off the couch and find somebody to talk to. Anyone—at this point the trash guy has more of a future than you do—at least everyone on your street misses him if he doesn't turn up.

I'm not suggesting you shun or abandon your negative friends; just make the decision to build relationships with people who are going where you want to go and need to go.

8. Actively engage in the admiration of others.

Let great men and women shape your life. Never graduate from hero worship. Never be too big or too proud to allow yourself to be inspired by the life struggles and victories of others.

You can cut your learning curve by up to 90% in anything you set out to accomplish by applying this strategy: learn from the experience of others.

Mimic the actions of those you know or read about. Learn from those people who continuously produce success and constantly overcome adversity.

This doesn't mean you should be awestruck by other people and try to copy them. Just because they have a TED talk doesn't make them better at being you, than you. Remember most people, despite their confident appearance and demeanor, are often just as scared and as doubtful of themselves as you are. Learn from their success, but apply it to <u>your</u> situation as only <u>you</u> can.

9. Actively cancel out any bad or negative thought.

Formulate and stamp indelibly on your mind a mental picture of yourself as succeeding. Hold this picture tenaciously. Never permit it to fade. Your mind will seek to develop this picture.

Never think of yourself as failing—never doubt the reality of the mental image. Doubting is the most dangerous thing you can do at this stage of the game. The mind always tries to complete the picture. So always picture success and victory for yourself, no matter how badly things seem to be going at the moment.

Fig. 12

10. Whatever you want.

I only had 9 points on my personal plan, but apparently to be a really successful self-help guru I would have to give up my last name and always have 10 points on all my lists.

So this is Dr. John signing off and wishing you unicorns and rainbows....

Seriously, you got this. If I can do this, so can you. If I can turn my complete cluster of a life around, so can you. I am not the cleverest guy on the planet, but I can be resilient, tenacious and persistent. I just got sick of being miserable all the time. So I cashed it all in, put it on black 13, and spun the wheel.

The result...my life is stinking AWESOME.

And I want nothing more than to see other people that have been written off and have written themselves off as losers have the AWESOMEREST life that they could ever imagine.

More from
DR. JOHN A. KING

Non-profit: www.givethemavoice.foundation

Books: www.thinkbigbooks.org

Speaking & Seminars: www.drjohnaking.com

For bookings or other information contact:
mel@nextfoundation.org

IMAGE CREDITS

Fig. 1 LilyRose97, Angry Cat. 2011, Digital Image. Available from: Flickr, https://www.flickr.com/photos/11747587@N08/14319102927 (accessed January 26, 2017). Words added.

Fig. 2 Sini Merikallio, Elephant Feet. 2012, Digital Image. Available from: Flickr, https://www.flickr.com/photos/smerikal/7634930564 (accessed January 20, 2017).

Fig. 3 Ryan McGuire, 256H. N.D., Digital Image. Available from: Gratisography, http://gratisography.com/#whimsical (accessed January 20, 2017).

Fig. 4 D.J., Human Brain on White Background. 2005, Digital Image. Available from: Flickr, https://www.flickr.com/photos/flamephoenix1991/8376271918 (accessed January 20, 2017).

Fig. 5 Kevan Davis, Work in Progress. 2011, Digital Image. Available from: Flickr, https://www.flickr.com/photos/kevandotorg/6229660191 (accessed January 20, 2017).

Fig. 6 J.J., Villainc. 2006, Digital Image. Available from: English Language Wikipedia, https://simple.wikipedia.org/wiki/Villain#/media/File:Villainc.svg (accessed January 20, 2017).

Fig. 7 Hyoin Min, Memory. 2012, Digital Illustration. Available from: Flickr, https://www.flickr.com/photos/nyoin/7933839082 (accessed January 20, 2017).

Fig. 8 Ryan McGuire, 141H. N.D., Digital Image. Available from: Gratisography, http://gratisography.com/#whimsical (accessed January 20, 2017).

Fig. 9 Skez, Dewey Bridge Fire. 2008, Digital Image. Available from English Language Wikipedia, https://commons.wikimedia.org/wiki/File:Dewey_Bridge_Fire_4-06-2008.jpg (accessed January 20, 2017).

Fig. 10 Matteo Staltari, Can you help me? There's a happy tomato in my mouth. 2010, Digital Image. Available from Flickr, https://www.flickr.com/photos/matteostaltari/5367134002/in/photostream/ (accessed January 20, 2017).

Fig. 11 Shoobydooby, Just Like a Ballerina. 2008, Digital Image. Available from Flickr, https://www.flickr.com/photos/shoobydooby/152619494 (accessed January 21, 2017) Words added.

Fig. 12 Monica, Unicorn. 2009, Digital Image. Available from Flickr, https://www.flickr.com/photos/scorpio58/4067099731 (accessed January 20, 2017). Words added.

Please note: Images with no assigned credit are either the author's own, purchased with licensing that requires no attribution, or public domain.

www.ingramcontent.com/pod-product-compliance
Lightning Source LLC
Chambersburg PA
CBHW070625300426
44113CB00010B/1660